Cat Club

Maine Coons

by Cameron L. Woodson

Bullfrog
Books

Ideas for Parents and Teachers

Bullfrog Books let children practice reading informational text at the earliest reading levels. Repetition, familiar words, and photo labels support early readers.

Before Reading
- Discuss the cover photo. What does it tell them?
- Look at the picture glossary together. Read and discuss the words.

Read the Book
- "Walk" through the book and look at the photos. Let the child ask questions. Point out the photo labels.
- Read the book to the child, or have him or her read independently.

After Reading
- Prompt the child to think more. Ask: Maine coons are large cats. Can you think of any other large cat breeds?

Bullfrog Books are published by Jump!
5357 Penn Avenue South
Minneapolis, MN 55419
www.jumplibrary.com

Library of Congress Cataloging-in-Publication Data

Names: Woodson, Cameron L., 1994– author.
Title: Maine coons / by Cameron L. Woodson.
Description: Bullfrog books edition.
Minneapolis: Jump!, Inc., [2021]
Series: Cat club | Includes index.
Audience: Ages 5–8 | Audience: Grades K–1
Identifiers: LCCN 2019048781 (print)
LCCN 2019048782 (ebook)
ISBN 9781645274490 (hardcover)
ISBN 9781645274506 (ebook)
Subjects: LCSH: Maine coon cat—Juvenile literature.
Classification: LCC SF449.M34 W66 2021 (print)
LCC SF449.M34 (ebook)
DDC 636.8/3—dc23
LC record available at https://lccn.loc.gov/2019048781
LC ebook record available at https://lccn.loc.gov/2019048782

Editors: Jenna Gleisner and Susanne Bushman
Designer: Jenna Casura

Photo Credits: Seregraff/Shutterstock, cover; GlobalP/iStock, 1, 8, 16b; Eric Isselee/Shutterstock, 3, 22; DenisNata/Shutterstock, 4, 9; Alexandra Jursova/Getty, 5, 23tr; Juniors Bildarchiv GmbH/Alamy, 6–7, 23bl; Grigoriy Pil/Shutterstock, 10–11, 23tl; Linn Currie/Shutterstock, 12–13, 23br; DragoNika/Shutterstock, 14–15; Nektarstock/iStock, 15; Yellow Cat/Shutterstock, 16t; Denys Prokofyev/Alamy, 17; VLADIMIR LVP/Shutterstock, 18–19; Happy monkey/Shutterstock, 20–21; Nynke van Holten/iStock, 24.

Printed in the United States of America at Corporate Graphics in North Mankato, Minnesota.

Table of Contents

Gentle Giants

This is a Maine coon!

These cats are big.

They are gentle.
They love people!

5

Maine coons
have long fur.

It makes a ruff.

ruff

Their fur can be many colors.

stripe

See the stripes?

tail

A long tail keeps
this cat warm.

It is bushy!

Nice!

Look at the ears.

See the tufts?

These keep them warm, too!

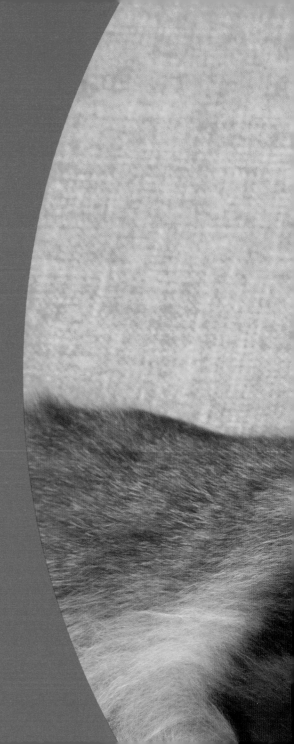

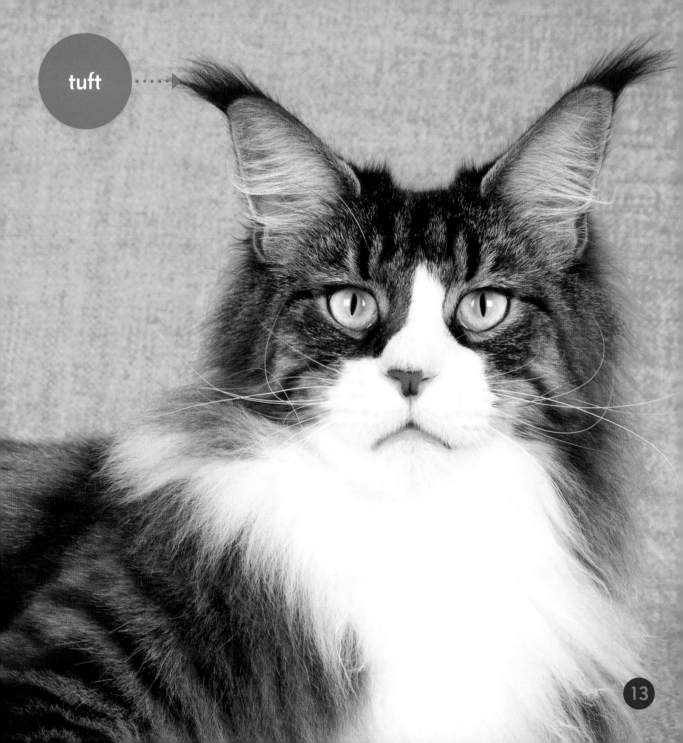

tuft

13

Their paws have tufts, too.
They help. How?
They can walk on snow!

paw

Maine coons love to play.

16

They like to be outside.

We take ours for a walk.

These cats love water.
Let's play in the sink!
Fun!

Do you want a Maine coon?

A Maine Coon Up Close

A Maine coon has long, fluffy fur. It has tufts on its ears and paws. Take a look at its other body parts!

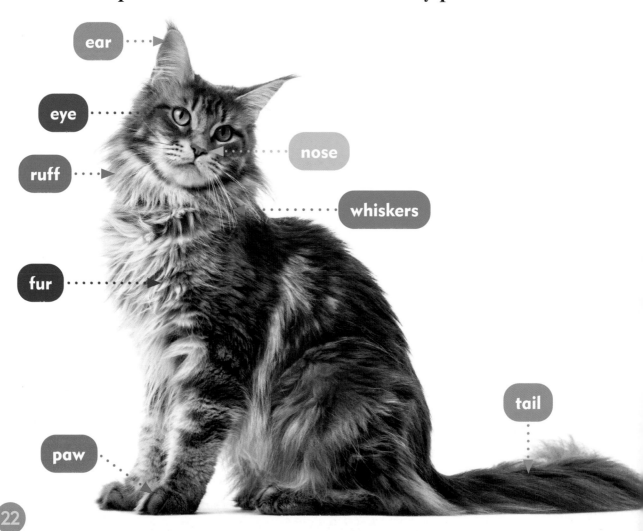

ear

eye

ruff

nose

whiskers

fur

tail

paw

Picture Glossary

bushy
Thick and spreading.

gentle
Not rough.

ruff
A collar of fur.

tufts
Bunches of hairs that are attached together at the bottom.

Index

To Learn More

Finding more information is as easy as 1, 2, 3.

❶ Go to www.factsurfer.com

❷ Enter "Mainecoons" into the search box.

❸ Click the "Surf" button to see a list of websites.